Mel Bay's Deluxe

MANUSCRIPT BOOK

featuring Tear-out Sheets

MEL BAY ®

PRACTICAL RANGES FOR INSTRUMENTS

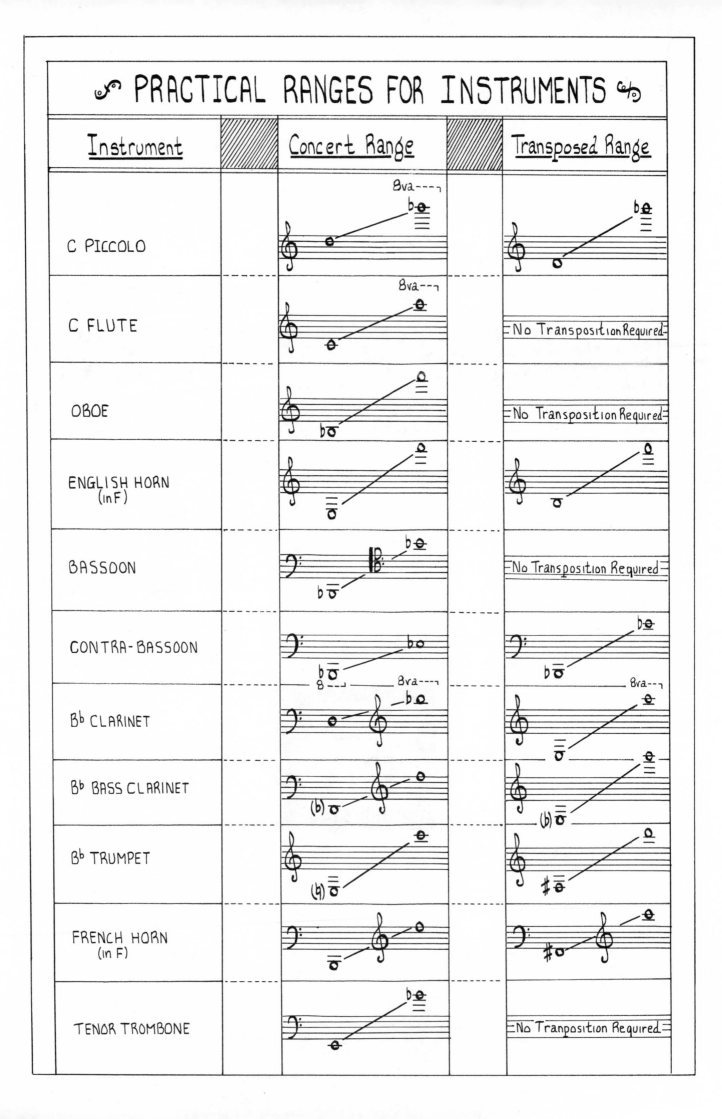

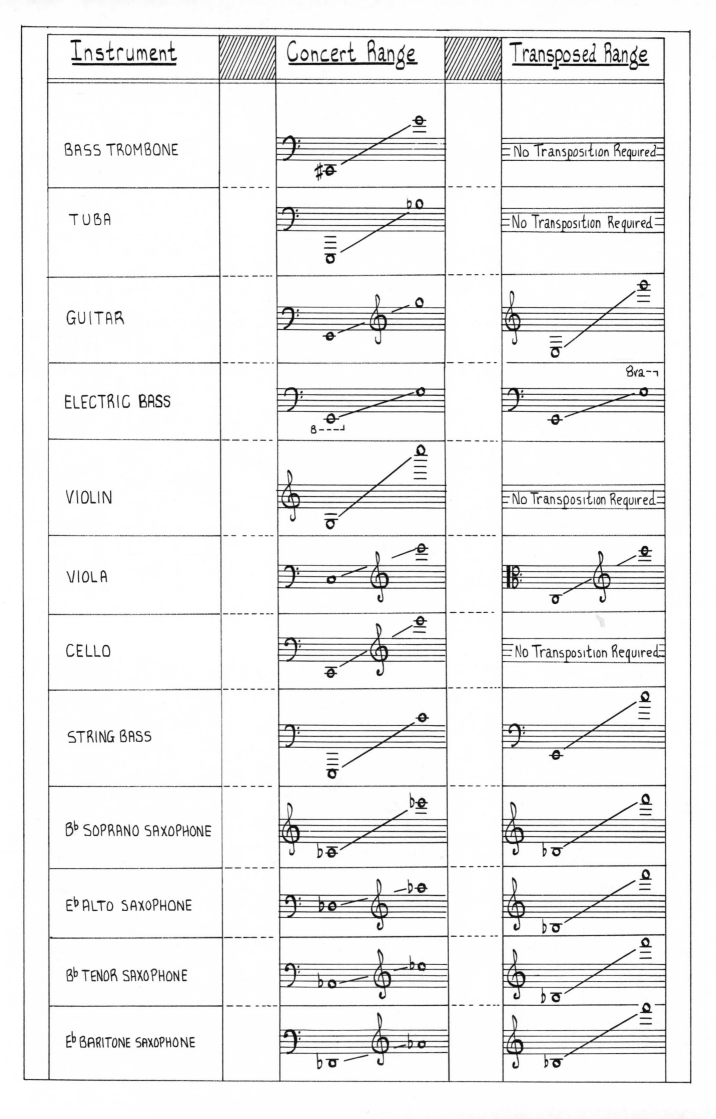

Chord Chart

Root	Major	Minor	Augmented	Diminished	Major 6	Major 7	Major 9
C	C	Cm	C+	C°	C6	Cmaj7	Cmaj9
F	F	Fm	F+	F°	F6	Fmaj7	Fmaj9
B♭	B♭	B♭m	B♭+	B♭°	B♭6	B♭maj7	B♭maj9
E♭	E♭	E♭m	E♭+	E♭°	E♭6	E♭maj7	E♭maj9
A♭	A♭	A♭m	A♭+	A♭°	A♭6	A♭maj7	A♭maj9
D♭	D♭	D♭m	D♭+	D♭°	D♭6	D♭maj7	D♭maj9
G♭	G♭	G♭m	G♭+	G♭°	G♭6	G♭maj7	G♭maj9
B	B	Bm	B+	B°	B6	Bmaj7	Bmaj9
E	E	Em	E+	E°	E6	Emaj7	Emaj9
A	A	Am	A+	A°	A6	Amaj7	Amaj9
D	D	Dm	D+	D°	D6	Dmaj7	Dmaj9
G	G	Gm	G+	G°	G6	Gmaj7	Gmaj9

Chord Chart

Minor 6	Minor 7	Minor 9	(Dominant) 7	(Dominant) 9	(Dominant) 11	(Dominant) 13	Dim. 7
Cm6	Cm7	Cm9	C7	C9	C11	C13	C°7
Fm6	Fm7	Fm9	F7	F9	F11	F13	F°7
B♭m6	B♭m7	B♭m9	B♭7	B♭9	B♭11	B♭13	B♭°7
E♭m6	E♭m7	E♭m9	E♭7	E♭9	E♭11	E♭13	E♭°7
A♭m6	A♭m7	A♭m9	A♭7	A♭9	A♭11	A♭13	A♭°7
D♭m6	D♭m7	D♭m9	D♭7	D♭9	D♭11	D♭13	D♭°7
G♭m6	G♭m7	G♭m9	G♭7	G♭9	G♭11	G♭13	G♭°7
Bm6	Bm7	Bm9	B7	B9	B11	B13	B°7
Em6	Em7	Em9	E7	E9	E11	E13	E°7
Am6	Am7	Am9	A7	A9	A11	A13	A°7
Dm6	Dm7	Dm9	D7	D9	D11	D13	D°7
Gm6	Gm7	Gm9	G7	G9	G11	G13	G°7

MAJOR SCALE

A MAJOR SCALE IS A SERIES OF EIGHT NOTES ARRANGED IN A PATTERN OF WHOLE STEPS AND HALF STEPS.

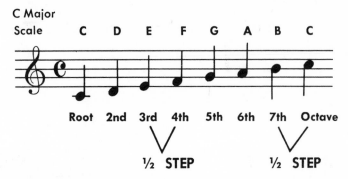

C to D	=	Whole Step
D to E	=	Whole Step
E to F	=	½ Step
F to G	=	Whole Step
G to A	=	Whole Step
A to B	=	Whole Step
B to C	=	½ Step

TO CONSTRUCT A MAJOR SCALE WE FIRST START WITH THE NAME OF THE SCALE (Frequently called the Root or Tonic). WITH THE C SCALE THIS WOULD BE THE NOTE "C". THE REST OF THE SCALE WOULD FALL IN LINE AS FOLLOWS:

G MAJOR SCALE

SCALE TONES		DISTANCE FROM PRECEDING NOTE
ROOT	(C)	
2nd	(D)	WHOLE STEP
3rd	(E)	WHOLE STEP
4th	(F)	½ STEP
5th	(G)	WHOLE STEP
6th	(A)	WHOLE STEP
7th	(B)	WHOLE STEP
Octave	(C)	½ STEP

TO CONSTRUCT THE G MAJOR SCALE, START WITH THE NOTE G, CONSTRUCT IT AS FOLLOWS:

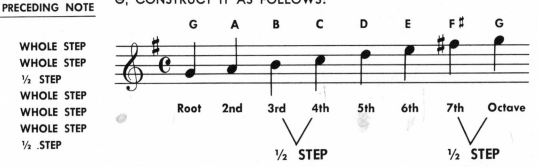

WITH THE ABOVE FORMULA YOU CAN CONSTRUCT ANY MAJOR SCALE!

NOTICE THAT IN ORDER TO MAKE OUR FORMULA WORK WITH THE G SCALE WE MUST SHARP (#) THE F. THERE MUST BE A WHOLE STEP BETWEEN THE 6th AND 7th TONES OF THE SCALE. IN ORDER TO ESTABLISH A WHOLE STEP BETWEEN E AND F WE MUST SHARP THE F.

MINOR SCALE

Many types of Minor Scales exist. For our purposes of chord construction, we will be dealing with the pure Minor Scale. The Formula for building a pure Minor Scale is as follows:

Find the 6th Tone of a Major Scale and continue through eight letters of that Major Scale. If we take the C Scale for example, we will find that A is the 6th Tone of the C Scale. If we then start with A and continue for eight notes, we will have the A Minor Scale.

"A" Minor is said to be "Relative" to C. (A is the 6th Tone in the C Scale and the A Minor Scale is built on the scale starting with A.)

MEL BAY PUBLICATIONS ● PACIFIC, MO. 63069

MEL BAY PUBLICATIONS ● PACIFIC, MO. 63069

MEL BAY PUBLICATIONS ● PACIFIC, MO. 63069

MEL BAY PUBLICATIONS ● PACIFIC, MO. 63069

MEL BAY PUBLICATIONS ● PACIFIC, MO. 63069

MEL BAY PUBLICATIONS ● PACIFIC, MO. 63069

MEL BAY PUBLICATIONS ● PACIFIC, MO. 63069

MEL BAY PUBLICATIONS • PACIFIC. MO. 63069

MEL BAY PUBLICATIONS · PACIFIC, MO. 63069

MEL BAY PUBLICATIONS ● PACIFIC, MO. 63069

MEL BAY PUBLICATIONS • PACIFIC, MO. 63069

MEL BAY PUBLICATIONS · PACIFIC, MO. 63069

MEL BAY PUBLICATIONS ● PACIFIC, MO. 63069

MEL BAY PUBLICATIONS ● PACIFIC, MO. 63069

MEL BAY PUBLICATIONS ● PACIFIC, MO. 63069

MEL BAY PUBLICATIONS • PACIFIC, MO. 63069

MEL BAY PUBLICATIONS ● PACIFIC, MO. 63069

MEL BAY PUBLICATIONS ● PACIFIC, MO. 63069

MEL BAY PUBLICATIONS ● PACIFIC, MO. 63069

MEL BAY PUBLICATIONS ● PACIFIC, MO. 63069

MEL BAY PUBLICATIONS • PACIFIC, MO. 63069

MEL BAY PUBLICATIONS ● PACIFIC, MO. 63069

MEL BAY PUBLICATIONS ● PACIFIC, MO. 63069